TEACHING
SOCIAL
STUDIES
to

TINA BEENE

Published by Seidlitz Education
P.O. Box 166827
Irving, TX 75016
www.seidlitzeducation.com

For related titles and support materials visit www.seidlitzeducation.com.

3.20

CONTENTS

CHAPTER 1
Introduction

I started teaching before I learned anything about how to actually teach. In fact, my alternative certification courses began the week after school started. I was living the nightmare scenario of building a plane while flying it, and I knew that fifty-five fifth-grade ELLs (English Language Learners) were depending on me not to crash and burn. I consoled myself with the knowledge that my more experienced teaching partner would be in charge of math and science, so at least my ineptitude could only do *so* much damage.

As a completely and utterly clueless first year teacher, I clung to the language arts and social studies textbooks I was given as though they were life-saving flotation devices. These manuals promised to guide me step-by-step as I taught my students and would surely mitigate any harms I might inadvertently inflict on them as a result of my ignorance.

Soon enough, as all teachers do, I began to find my "groove" as it pertained to language arts instruction. I have always had a passion for literacy and made it my life's ambition to pass on that love to my students. If there were an ELA (English Language Arts) or SLA (Spanish Language Arts) training course offered in my district, I was there. If a new book came out about engaging reluctant readers, I bought it. As my mother would say, my students were going to love reading, whether they liked it or not.

And yet, at the same time, it would be generous to say that my social studies lessons were less than inspiring. Eventually I knew I could only ask my students to "Read Section Two of Chapter Three and choose two questions from the section review to answer" a few more times before I had a mutiny on my hands. Why weren't my students eager to learn about the past? Why didn't they see the connections between their own lives and the events covered in our textbook? How could a content so nuanced, so fraught with both human folly and glory, be perceived by my students to be so, well, boring?

> "Scaffolding is the temporary assistance by which a teacher helps a learner know how to do something so that the learner will later be able to complete a similar task alone. It is future-oriented and aimed at increasing a learner's autonomy."
>
> Gibbons (2015)

The first step in the right direction was discovered at the back of yet another cabinet my room's previous tenant (or previous seven, given the state of the room) had not bothered to clean out before relocating. *History Alive!* was scrawled across the spine of a set of thin, navy textbooks. That's all I needed to see, since I was: 1) desperate for new resources and 2) especially interested in ones that promised to resuscitate my students' enjoyment of social studies.

That resource transformed the way I taught social studies, there's no question about it. My students began to look forward to the days when the blue books appeared, and so did I. They were engaged, invested, and able to easily make connections to their lives from the content. Yet over time, I began to realize not all of my students were responding so positively. While most of them were really "getting" what *History Alive!* had to offer, their enthusiasm was masking a dismaying truth: this silver bullet wasn't working for ALL of my students. I became frustrated and set off to find another approach. Every now and again I would catch a glimpse of those distinctive blue spines and think back wistfully to the times my students had been fired up about creating the best possible propaganda poster for their colonies or had designed their own settlers, but mostly I just felt like a gigantic failure. What was I missing? Why didn't such a great resource work for all "my" kids? What could I have done differently?

I now know that what my students needed was scaffolding to access the valuable content. According to Gibbons (2015), "Scaffolding is the temporary assistance by which a teacher helps a learner know how to do something so that the learner will later be able to complete a similar task alone. It is future-oriented and aimed at increasing a learner's autonomy." Just like the literal scaffolding that is placed around a building during construction, instructional scaffolding is removed and repositioned as each phase is completed.

However, even if I had known about scaffolding as an instructional practice and had used it with the textbook, that alone would not have been sufficient to increase the academic achievement of my ELLs. I needed to better understand how to provide that support on a daily basis, regardless of the resource at hand. I needed to consider how many of my students spent their previous academic careers learning different geography, and how many had an understanding of major historical events from a completely different perspective. I needed to be aware of the unique experiences in their lives that had led them to this classroom, and how many of the main concepts of our content (e.g. push and pull factors) they might understand, but not be able to express because of their lack of English proficiency.

USING THIS BOOK

Chapters 2, 3, and 4 include class activities that will engage ELLs and strengthen comprehension.

Look for the friendly teacher speech bubbles with suggested questions that will help focus student thinking.

I know now that what I was seeking (both as classroom teacher and later as a support for classroom teachers) was an explicit and practical guide to supporting my ELLs in each component of the typical social studies lesson and at each stage of language proficiency that respected the ideas, beliefs, and experiences they brought to the classroom.

Eventually I left the classroom for an instructional coaching position and then moved into several different roles at the district office. As I began to work with more and more teachers, I realized they were exactly where I had been; they had a general understanding of "why" differentiation is necessary for ELLs and a surface knowledge of "how" to go about it, but when it came time to ascribe specific accommodations to real lessons, they often got stuck. That's when we would work together through every minute of a single lesson, choosing activities and resources that would build the most language while making the content comprehensible for all students. And it worked.

This resource is designed around that tried-and-true format. It features chapters dedicated to each of the most common lesson components found in social studies classrooms today: warm-ups; building background; direct instruction; academic reading, writing, and conversations; and finally, assessment. Each chapter explores the instructional role of that component, the challenges ELLs often face in that portion of the lesson, the ways in which they benefit from that aspect of the lesson, and strategies tailored to the component to maximize learning for ELLs at all proficiency levels.

In whatever way you utilize this book, whether it's reading it cover-to-cover or zeroing in on scaffolded strategies for a component that has proven difficult, my hope is that this resource will assist you in remaining mindful of your ELLs throughout your lesson planning and delivery. The goal of this book is to share detailed analyses of how and why we do what we do in the social studies classroom alongside strategies designed specifically for your ELLs that will maximize achievement for all of your students, and to do so in a way that reflects and respects your current classroom practices.

CHALLENGES POSED BY THE LANGUAGE OF SOCIAL STUDIES

It is challenging for students to acquire academic content and the English language at the same time, regardless of the content area. However, the relative complexity and unfamiliarity of both the content and the language through which it is conveyed pose additional difficulties in social studies that may not be as pronounced in other content areas.

Vocabulary

Students are often exposed to some rather complex ideas for the first time (socialism vs. communism, for example) using vocabulary that is equally unfamiliar.

General Academic Vocabulary	*event, evidence, cause*
Culture-Specific Vocabulary	*pioneer, frontier, rebel*
Culturally-Biased Vocabulary	*savage, hordes, mob, fanatic*
Specialized Vocabulary	*monarchy, revolution, slavery*

(Suzanne Irujo, Boston University CONNTesol, November 7, 2009)

Grammatical Structures

As students learn English, the first messages they understand and begin to reproduce are generally spoken and written in the present tense, using highly familiar vocabulary about simple topics. Often, the language of social studies is none of those things and that can make comprehension a challenge, especially for beginner and intermediate ELLs.

Passive and Impersonal Structures	*…crops such as coffee, cotton, and tobacco are cultivated by resident labor…*
Verb Tenses	*How might his experiences as a backwoodsman have helped him become a successful leader?*
Unclear References	*Jim told Andy that Dr. Scott suspected that he cheated on the history exam.*
Complex Embedded Clauses	*He explored a large area of what was to become the Southeastern United States, including present-day…*
Hypothetical Past Conditions	*What might have happened to the colonists on Roanoke Island?*

(Suzanne Irujo, Boston University CONNTesol, November 7, 2009)

Language Functions and Structures for Conversation

Moving past the words and the structures that are used to communicate them, students also face the challenge of engaging with the language of social studies in a meaningful way so that they can discuss key concepts in the academic register.

Abstract Cognitively Demanding Concepts	*democracy, representation, inequality, bias, propaganda*
Functions	*describe, explain, interpret, identify cause/ effect, draw conclusions*
Discourse Markers	*initially, subsequently, ultimately, finally, as a result, consequently, therefore, in order to, similarly, equally, whereas, on the other hand, unlike, however, although*

Given these challenges, how do I help ELLs develop social studies language?

Students develop social studies language in much the same way as they master language in other situations: through substantial practice in highly engaging and low- stress environments (Lee & VanPatten, 2003). Therefore, it is not necessary for us to directly teach each of the facets of language noted above. It is important for us as teachers to be aware of these challenges so that we can best support students. But from their perspective, the most important thing we can do is expose them to the language with opportunities to practice it themselves. As the saying goes, *If students don't verbalize, students don't internalize,* and students are most willing to do so in an environment that promotes risk-taking and encourages them to make mistakes as they progress in their language and content knowledge. When given consistent opportunities to engage in structured interactions and to "show what they know" through scaffolded academic tasks, students will acquire both the content and the language of social studies at a remarkable pace.

CHAPTER 2
Setting the Stage

✔ Warm-Ups

✔ Building Background

By maintaining records of the people, places, and events that shaped its history, a society is able to retain the knowledge that has been gained over time and benefit from the wisdom of those who have gone before. If the young people in a society are to benefit from that shared knowledge, they must have an understanding of both how and why things came to be the way they are at the present moment.

However, it can be quite challenging to provide students with a robust understanding of social studies when they lack common background experiences or shared cultural norms. As social studies teachers, we must not only teach students about the history of the world and of American society in particular, but also teach them how the people, places, and events that have been preserved for posterity have influenced modern society.

So how exactly can one teacher accomplish this with a classroom of students with varying levels of background knowledge and English language proficiency? In this book, we will explore how we can engage all students through each component of a standard social studies lesson, while providing the scaffolding and opportunities to develop background knowledge that ELLs often need to be successful.

WARM-UPS

A warm-up, often called a "bell-ringer," is a short activity designed to get students settled, cognitively engaged, and ready for whatever you have to share with them that day. It can be a quick review of previously covered content or an invitation to speculate about something new to be covered. It is often an invitation to access prior knowledge students have about the topic. It can be an individual, partner, or group endeavor.

Sometimes we overlook the importance of the warm-up, eager to "get the day started" and move on to new content. However, for your ELLs and your reluctant learners, the warm-up often impacts how they learn for the remainder of the class. If it's too challenging, or if it's perceived as busywork, students who struggle may give up before they even begin.

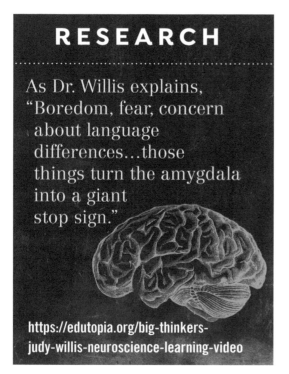

RESEARCH

As Dr. Willis explains, "Boredom, fear, concern about language differences...those things turn the amygdala into a giant stop sign."

https://edutopia.org/big-thinkers-judy-willis-neuroscience-learning-video

Many ELLs, especially beginner and intermediate students, rely on routines and procedures to help them navigate the barrage of language they encounter during the school day. If the opening minutes of your class are chaotic or unpredictable, this can create stress for your students. Research summarized by Dr. Judy Willis tells us that students who are stressed or scared (or even bored!) are unable to learn. Experiencing the "fight, flight, or freeze" impulse prevents the brain from successfully analyzing higher-order questions and tasks, and also precludes students from storing information long term.

A properly designed warm-up brings all of your students to the metaphorical table. If it offers a preview of what is to come, then it provides crucial context for ELLs. If it invites students to share their experiences, ideas, or opinions, it shows respect for them as individuals. If it "teases" interesting material ahead, it builds engagement and anticipation.

Uncover the Picture

The teacher presents an image on PowerPoint or via document camera that is completely covered. The image is uncovered slowly while students list things they see. The teacher pauses three times to let students make predictions about the image.

What do you see?

Where could this be?

When might this photograph have been taken?

What else do you see in the image now?

What do you think you'll see in the final section of the photograph?

What surprised you about the second and third sections of this photograph?

What questions do you have now that you've seen the entire photograph?

South China Sea 4/3/1975. Crewmen of the amphibious cargo ship USS Durham (LKA-114) take Vietnamese refugees aboard a small craft. The refugees will be transferred later by mechanized landing craft (LCM) to the freighter Transcolorado. General Records of the Department of the Navy, National Archives Identifier 558518.

NEWCOMER/BEGINNER	INTERMEDIATE	ADVANCED	NEARLY FLUENT
Students identify items using a native language resource.	Students identify items and add descriptor.	Students identify items, add how and why.	Students identify items/ideas; make predictions.
I see a...	*I noticed a...*	*It is significant that ____ because...*	*I'm wondering ____ because...*

Language Anticipation Guide
(Head & Readence, 1986)

Students are presented with academic terms and phrases that will be discussed in the day's lesson alongside possible definitions of the terms. Students select whether the stated definition (e.g. "the word 'interest' means something that you like or enjoy doing") is the true definition for the way the term is being used in the day's lesson. After instruction, students revisit their initial predictions of what the words meant to see if they need to adjust any of their predictions.

1. Select 3-8 key words or phrases found in a social studies passage.

2. Write a true/false statement for each key word that focuses on the meaning of the word as it is used in the passage. This set of statements becomes the Language Anticipation Guide.

3. Have students examine the statements and decide if the statements are true or false, prior to reading. This may be done individually, but it is a great opportunity for pairs to have an academic discussion as well.

4. Have students read the passage, taking note of the context surrounding each word from the Language Anticipation Guide.

5. Have students make changes to their true/false choices in light of any new understandings they formed while reading.

6. Conduct a brief, whole-group discussion for each Language Anticipation Guide statement.

The Gettysburg Address

STATEMENT	BEFORE READING	AFTER READING
The word *score* means how many points each team has at the end of the game.	TRUE | FALSE	TRUE | FALSE
The word *vain* describes someone who thinks too highly of himself, especially about his appearance.	TRUE | FALSE	TRUE | FALSE
The word *ground* means to attach something to the floor.	TRUE | FALSE	TRUE | FALSE

Four score and seven years ago our fathers brought forth on this continent a new nation, conceived in liberty, and dedicated to the proposition that all men are created equal.

Now we are engaged in a great civil war, testing whether that nation, or any nation so conceived and so dedicated, can long endure. We are met on a great battlefield of that war. We have come to dedicate a portion of that field, as a final resting place for those who here gave their lives that that nation might live. It is altogether fitting and proper that we should do this.

But, in a larger sense, we can not dedicate, we can not consecrate, we can not hallow this ground. The brave men, living and dead, who struggled here, have consecrated it, far above our poor power to add or detract. The world will little note, nor long remember what we say here, but it can never forget what they did here. It is for us the living, rather, to be dedicated here to the unfinished work which they who fought here have thus far so nobly advanced. It is rather for us to be here dedicated to the great task remaining before us—that from these honored dead we take increased devotion to that cause for which they gave the last full measure of devotion—that we here highly resolve that these dead shall not have died in vain—that this nation, under God, shall have a new birth of freedom—and that government of the people, by the people, for the people, shall not perish from the earth.

NEWCOMER/BEGINNER	INTERMEDIATE	ADVANCED	NEARLY FLUENT
Students complete 1-2 items from each column using a native-language resource for support. *I choose (true/false) for number 1.*	Students complete both columns with teacher support as needed for non-key terms. They discuss any adjustments made to "before" statements using the stem: *I chose (true/false) for number ___, but now I think...*	Students complete both Before and After columns with minimal assistance. They discuss any adjustments made to "before" predictions after reading using the stem: *At first I thought number ___ was (true /false) but now I think ____ because...*	Students complete both Before and After columns without assistance. They discuss any adjustments made to "before" predictions after reading using the stem: *After reading, I changed my answer on number ___ to (true/false) based on...*

Prediction Café *(Zwiers, 2008)*

Students use many critical thinking skills such as predicting, inferring, and synthesizing in this activity. The teacher selects quotes, headings, and captions from a text and writes them on cards. Students read/discuss their cards in rotating partnerships, making predictions about the upcoming text/lesson based on their cards. Students are expected to use academic language as they converse.

1. Select important headings, quotations, or captions (about eight per class) from the text that students will read. Put them on separate index cards. Prepare one for each student. Even though some students will receive the same card, their predictions will vary.

2. Display the title of the text for all students to see.

3. Explain the goal of the activity: to make predictions about the main idea OR the author's purpose for the text.

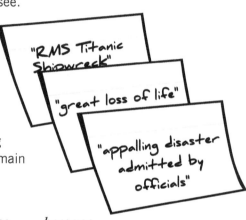

4. Give each student a card. Have students form pairs.

5. Have students read the cards individually and make a prediction or guess about the meaning of the quotation as it relates to the predicted main idea/purpose of the overall text.

6. Provide stems to facilitate discussion,

   _____ *makes me think that...*   *I believe _____ because...*

   I predict the main idea is...   *I think the author's purpose is...*

7. Have the second partner share his/her sentence cards in the same way, and then have the partners discuss what they think the main idea of the text will be.

8. Have students find a different partner and repeat the process. Student predictions about the main idea should improve as they hear more and more quotations and predictions from other students.

9. Bring the class back together and lead a brief discussion about student predictions.

NEWCOMER/BEGINNER	INTERMEDIATE	ADVANCED	NEARLY FLUENT
Students read a simple caption to each of their partners. *My card says... What does yours say?*	After clarification of pronunciation of key terms, students complete this activity without further accommodation. *My card says____, so I predict...*	Students use stems with past, present, and future tenses. *According to my card, (reads card); therefore, my prediction was...*	Students use stems with past, present, future tenses, and complex grammar. *Based on this (caption, quote, heading) that said____, it is my prediction that____ (will/will not) ____.*

The authors of the SIOP (Sheltered Instruction Observation Protocol) model discuss three key components in building background (Echevarria, Vogt, & Short, 2008). They include: accessing prior knowledge, linking to prior learning experiences, and exposing students to new vocabulary and language. Each of these components necessitates that students bring outside information into the classroom. In addition, the teacher provides students with linguistic and conceptual understandings necessary to participate fully in a learning experience.

No other content area understands the importance of building background knowledge quite like social studies. Even students who have lived their entire lives in the same city may have very different levels of understanding about both current and historical events. This is even more true for ELLs who might have been born and raised for some portion of their childhood in a different country. Regardless of their upbringing, each of your students brings a unique understanding of the world to your classroom each day, one that is colored by their own cultural background and experiences. Instead of viewing that disparity as a challenge, we can choose to view it as an opportunity to draw from each student's perspective to create a richer understanding of the world around us while fostering a respectful classroom community. Well-designed activities for building background invite newcomer ELLs to contribute their voices and share their unique perspectives.

Building background often occurs in our classrooms as "in the moment" asides where the teacher attempts to bring students up to speed regarding a topic the teacher assumed students would not need to be directly taught. This impromptu deviation from the expected lesson can leave ELLs confused. It can also be challenging for the teacher to remember to speak slowly and clearly and to minimize the use of figurative language while trying to convey this new idea.

No other content area understands the importance of building background knowledge quite like social studies.

Let's examine how some pre-planning for building background can positively impact achievement for your ELLs.

Imagine a teacher standing in front of her eighth-grade class, presenting a lesson designed for the following standard: *Identify selected racial, ethnic, and religious groups that settled in the United States and explain their reasons for immigration.* She has taken time to compile authentic resources such as diary entries, film footage, and photographs from Ellis Island to help her students connect with the lesson. She has led students through an engaging warm-up to get them ready for the new material, and has encouraged them to imagine themselves facing the challenge of immigrating to a new country and the motivation they might have to do so. As the lesson progresses, she has several thought-provoking exchanges with some of her most eager students. At the end of the lesson, students complete an exit ticket that shows that the majority of students grasped the key concepts and are more informed than they were when class began. Her two beginner ELLs even completed the sentence "I came from _____" as both their tickets and the teacher feels the day has been a success.

Now imagine the same teacher doing that same lesson, but this time she brings her newcomer ELLs along for the ride. Instead of introducing them to the topic alongside the rest of the class, she has been working with them here and there the last two weeks, whenever she could, to learn their stories. She has asked simple, engaging questions about their past, writing them down for the students to translate and then assisting them with their responses. By the time she introduces her Ellis Island lesson, she has an authentic paragraph from each newcomer to share with the class. Instead of starting with black and white photographs and diary entries from decades ago, she begins the lesson by displaying and reading aloud the paragraphs the newcomers have carefully prepared. This time, all the students are engaged. The newcomers have contributed in a meaningful way while providing an opportunity for their classmates to see how relevant the topic is to each of them. This time, when she shares her authentic resources, she and her students draw connections between immigration then and now. The discussion is more lively, more nuanced, and more inclusive. The students' exit tickets reflect a deeper understanding of the topic and they have their ELL classmates to thank.

As teachers of ELLs, we can transform our ELLs into assets instead of observers in our classrooms. We can celebrate the diversity they bring to the room and the opportunities they present for us to consider other cultures, other ways, even other versions of historical events. We can use their stories as a springboard to help each student discover his or her own narrative, to explore how and why things came to be the way that they are. We can, in essence, bring history to life.

List, Group, Label *(Taba, 1967)*

Students organize vocabulary in a variety of ways to gain a deeper understanding of academic terms to help them clarify the relationships between academic concepts and the meaning of academic terms. Students write key terms on individual cards and then sort the terms into group-generated categories such as topic, characteristic, etc.

1. Give students a list of words, or have students brainstorm a list of words related to a given academic topic.

2. Ask students to copy the words or terms onto index cards with one word per card. Students can complete this step in groups.

3. Have students discuss the words and organize them into piles based on similarities. Each pile must have at least two cards.

4. Have students create a label for each pile that explains how the words within that pile are similar. Students might label by topic, by part of speech, by characteristic, etc.

5. Have students compare their labels to see how other groups organize the same information.

After finishing a unit on the Great Depression, the teacher and class might generate the following list:

Black Tuesday	Public Works program
deficit	Wagner Act
Hoovervilles	social security system
Dust Bowl	Huey Long
Bonus Army	Dorothea Lange
speculation	
New Deal	

After discussing and sorting, students might generate categories such as: outcomes of the Depression, causes of the Depression, key figures during the Depression, etc.

NEWCOMER/BEGINNER	INTERMEDIATE	ADVANCED	NEARLY FLUENT
Students utilize a native-language resource to find equivalent terms for the academic terms on the cards, placing the English term and a picture on one side and the native language equivalent on the other side. The students then listen to the group discussion, sorting their own cards accordingly.	After clarification of pronunciation of key terms, students share at least one idea during the group discussion.	Students are able to explain the reasoning for the categories generated using correct sentence structure and grammar. *We elected to create the category of ____ because...*	Students are able to explain the reasoning for the categories generated using correct sentence structure and grammar. *We elected to create the category of ____ because...*

Search and Share

Students are given three minutes to gather as much information as possible (in any language) regarding the day's topic. They then share with their group, compiling a list of all of their answers. This is then followed by a whole class Whip Around.

During Whip Around, one person from each group stands and holds their group's list of compiled information. One at a time, each group shares one item from their list. Every other group marks off what has been shared so that no answers are repeated. Groups sit down when all of their answers have been shared. The activity ends when all groups are seated.

NEWCOMER/BEGINNER	INTERMEDIATE	ADVANCED	NEARLY FLUENT
Students read independently about the topic in their native language, complete a Quick Draw (see p. 23) to show one idea from the reading, and listen to the group and class discussions.	Students read independently about the topic in their native language, English, or a combination of both. They share at least one idea in the group discussion, utilizing the following stem: *One thing I read about (the topic) was ____.*	Students read independently in English and have 3-5 items to share at the end of the time limit. *I discovered_____.*	Students read independently in English and have 3-5 items to share at the end of the time limit. *I discovered_____.*

Describe, Describe, Draw

(Adpated from Marzano, 2004; Seidlitz, Base, Lara, & Smith, 2016)

The teacher describes a vocabulary term to students, making sure to use visuals and student-friendly language to increase comprehension. Students then describe the term in pairs or small groups. Ideas are shared out with the whole group. Students then work individually or in pairs to create a drawing that represents the meaning of the term, the main idea, or a connection or association the student has made.

1. Describe a vocabulary term to students.
2. Have students describe the term with a partner or in groups.
3. Have students draw a representation of the term.

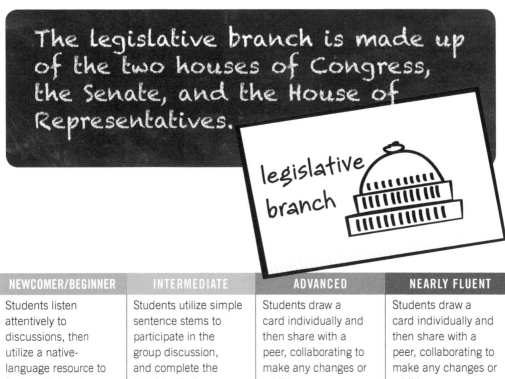

NEWCOMER/BEGINNER	INTERMEDIATE	ADVANCED	NEARLY FLUENT
Students listen attentively to discussions, then utilize a native-language resource to find equivalent terms for the academic terms being discussed. They then draw the English term and a picture on one side and the native language equivalent on the other side.	Students utilize simple sentence stems to participate in the group discussion, and complete the individual/pair discussion with assistance from native-language peer/resource as needed. *I drew a _____ because...*	Students draw a card individually and then share with a peer, collaborating to make any changes or additions.	Students draw a card individually and then share with a peer, collaborating to make any changes or additions.

CHAPTER 3
Content Delivery

✔ Interactive Lecture

✔ Academic Reading

S tudent engagement with social studies material can be effectively fostered through interactive lectures and academic reading. As you present an interactive lecture, students are encouraged to actively participate rather than to simply listen. Academic reading allows students to make sense of various source materials and produce language output that illustrates what they've learned.

INTERACTIVE LECTURE

A lecture becomes interactive when students are given the opportunity to engage with the information as it is being presented. Instead of being passive recipients, they are actively constructing knowledge as the lesson progresses. This means they are listening, speaking, reading, and writing, of course, but most importantly, they are *thinking*.
This makes it much more likely that the crucial information being presented will

The interactive lecture portion of your daily instruction is probably the instructional component that least resembles the way you were taught as a secondary student. Gone are the days of droning lectures and pages of handwritten notes. Educators have come to realize that students learn best when the information is "chunked" into comprehensible pieces so that they are given time to process the information they are receiving. There will always be a need for teachers to share their knowledge directly with students, and the ability to take notes during a lecture is a crucial life skill for students who pursue higher education. These strategies will help keep students focused and will increase their retention of the information that is being shared.

For ELLs, it can be difficult to attend to spoken language for more than a few minutes. While it may seem like the teacher is doing most of the work during a lecture, ELLs at the lower proficiency levels are facing extreme cognitive demand as they decipher the words being spoken. It does not help that we often pepper our lecture with asides, idioms, and figurative language that can leave students feeling lost.

One of the primary benefits of an interactive lecture is that it gives students an opportunity to clarify, connect, and express their understanding of the information being presented at the same time the information is being delivered. By designing the lecture this way, the teacher allows students to pause, process, and internalize the information "in the moment," which makes it more meaningful, and also increases the likelihood that the information will be retained.

Turn and Tell Five
(Seidlitz & Perryman, 2010a)

What did your partner tell you?

Is there anything you would add to what your partner shared?

During the lecture, students are prompted to turn and tell a partner what is being discussed for approximately five seconds.

A student is then chosen randomly to share out.

NEWCOMER/BEGINNER	INTERMEDIATE	ADVANCED	NEARLY FLUENT
Students speak to a native-language peer, or an English-speaking peer who is comfortable working with a beginner.	Students share with a native-language partner if possible, and likely use a mix of English and native language. *We are discussing...*	Students use a variety of grammatical structures to discuss with a partner. *Today we are discussing ____ because....*	Students use a variety of grammatical structures to discuss with a partner. *Today we are discussing ____ because....*

Point and Talk *(Seidlitz, Base, Lara, & Smith, 2016)*

Before class, the teacher previews the lesson and identifies which directions will be given orally and what key concepts will be discussed. The teacher then plans what objects he/she will hold, refer to, or use as models. While delivering the content, the teacher makes eye contact with students of lower language proficiency levels and occasionally uses questions and response signals to measure understanding of both the content and directions.

"On a scale of 1-5, how well do you understand what is being shared right now?"

"Can you and your neighbor think of any words I might need to explain again?"

NEWCOMER/BEGINNER	INTERMEDIATE	ADVANCED	NEARLY FLUENT
Students are instructed in their native language to utilize a series of signals to the teacher to indicate when they need a slower pace or when they would like to talk to a native-language peer or use a resource. Signals such as forming a T with their hands for a time-out to clarify are helpful.	Students use the 1-5 scale when the teacher asks for feedback. They are also prompted to ask for clarification when needed.	Students use the 1-5 scale when the teacher asks for feedback. They are also prompted to ask for clarification when needed.	Students use the 1-5 scale when the teacher asks for feedback. They are also prompted to ask for clarification when needed.

Quick Draw

After a key idea has been presented, students are given one minute to quickly sketch a representation of the idea that is then shared with a partner. Finally, a student is chosen randomly to share out before additional volunteers are allowed to share.

What prompted you to draw what you drew?

Did anyone else's drawing help you understand the word?

NEWCOMER/BEGINNER	INTERMEDIATE	ADVANCED	NEARLY FLUENT
Students use a native-language resource and/or peer to complete their sketches.	Students utilize simple sentence stems to discuss their drawings with peers, utilizing native-language peer/resource as needed. *I drew a _____ because...*	Students complete the task individually and then share with a peer, collaborating to make any changes or additions.	Students complete the task individually and then share with a peer, collaborating to make any changes or additions.

As Nancy Motley (2016) explains in *Talk, Read, Talk, Write*, academic reading is an active process wherein students gain knowledge through reading. Sources for this may include current news clippings, a primary source from centuries ago, or a fictionalized account of a historic event, for example. Students read alone, in pairs, or in groups to deepen their understanding or to learn new material.

Engaging in academic reading allows students to examine multiple perspectives, to explore the world from another place and time, and to deepen their understanding about historical events. While reading in the content areas is important to every discipline, it is absolutely critical in the social studies classroom.

TYPES OF SOCIAL STUDIES READING

Historical Retelling	Reports past events in a logical sequence
Historical Account	Accounts for how and/or why past events happened in a particular order
Historical Explanation	Explains past events in terms of causes and consequences
Historical Argument	Advocates for a particular perspective or position regarding a historical event

Adapted from Schleppegrell, *The Language of Schooling* (2004)

Input from a new language is received in two ways: listening and reading. According to the Oxford English Dictionary, there are approximately 170,000 words currently used in the English language. Yet when we speak, we most frequently use the same 3,000 words. If we want our students to develop robust vocabularies, it is imperative they spend time reading social studies texts in our classroom. While interactive lectures are engaging and effective, students will not develop the language necessary to be successful academically—especially in terms of standardized assessments—if academic reading is not utilized alongside our spoken messages.

When we encourage students to learn through reading for themselves instead of transmitting the information verbally to them, we allow them to make their own connections and derive meaning that is not connected to our own interpretation of the information. However, some students are adept at what Motley calls "pretend engagement," some students are several grade levels below the target reading level, and some students have developed a general disinterest in literacy. Each of these challenges necessitates the implementation of strategies to keep students focused on the task at hand.

Adapted/Native Language Text

Students read a text that is scaffolded for their particular proficiency level, then discuss their reading with a partner.

for advanced/nearly fluent

And the Shots Rang Out!
(Seidlitz & Perryman, 2010b)

For eighteen months the tension between the citizens of Boston and His Majesty's Red Coat soldiers had been mounting. Their arrival on September 30, 1768, was not a welcome event. The soldiers had traveled to Boston to enforce the Townsend Acts and to police the colonists, not protect them. Citizens of Boston were forced to quarter these soldiers.

On the night of March 5, 1770, three angry mobs assembled on King Street near the State House and Custom's House. The Custom's House was where the taxes were being collected.

One lone soldier by the name of Hugh White was guarding the Custom's House that evening.

The angry mob began taunting the soldier. Snowballs and insults were being directed toward the soldier. Several more Red Coat soldiers appeared to assist White. The angry mob continued their harassment of the red coats soldiers. One mob participant took a club or stick and struck one of the soldiers by the name of Hugh Montgomery. Some say it was Crispus Attucks who did the deed.

The bells of Boston began ringing that night. Many Bostonians fetched their buckets, as the bells were often an indication of a fire.

Suddenly, the word "fire" could be heard near the riotous mob. The soldiers raised their musket guns and fired into the angry crowd.

Three people were killed immediately, two more would die later from their wounds. The event became known as the Boston Massacre. Afterward, Paul Revere's engraved print of the Boston Massacre entitled; The Bloody Massacre Perpetrated on King Street, fueled the flames of discontent among the American colonists.

Adapted/Native Language Text *continued*

for intermediate

And the Shots Rang Out! (adapted text)
(Seidlitz & Perryman, 2010b)

The British soldiers argued with the citizens of Boston for a long time. The soldiers arrived on September 30, 1768. They came to Boston to make the colonists obey the Townsend Acts which were taxes and rules the colonists did not want to obey because they thought they were unjust. The citizens of Boston had to let the soldiers stay in their houses even though they did not like them.

On the night of March 5, 1770, an angry group of young men were standing on King Street, near the Customs House in Boston. The Customs House was the place where the British collected taxes. There was a British soldier named Hugh White who was protecting the Customs House that night.

The angry group of young men insulted the soldier and threw snowballs at him. Several more Red Coat soldiers appeared to assist White. One of the young men struck one of the British soldiers with a stick. The bells of Boston churches started ringing to warn the people of danger. Many of the people in Boston grabbed buckets because they thought the ringing bells meant there was a fire. The British soldiers heard someone in the crowd shout, "Fire!" The soldiers raised their guns, called muskets, and fired into the group of angry young men. Three of the young men died right there and two died later. They called the event, "The Boston Massacre." The event made the colonists angrier with the British.

What information from
your reading should you bring up in
conversation with your partner?

What is one thing your partner
noticed about the reading?

¡Y Los Tiros Se Escucharon!
(Spanish translation of adapted text)
(Seidlitz & Perryman, 2010b)

Los soldados británicos alegaron con los ciudadanos de Boston por un largo tiempo. Los soldados llegaron el 30 de septiembre de 1768. Vinieron a Boston para asegurar que los colonos respetaran la ley de Townsend, la cual imponía impuestos y reglas que los colonos no querían obedecer porque pensaban que eran injustas. Los ciudadanos de Boston eran forzados a alojar a los soldados en sus casas a pesar de que no les agradaban.

En la noche del 5 de marzo de 1770, un grupo de hombres jóvenes se encontraban reunidos en la calle King, cerca de la casa aduanal en Boston. Los jóvenes estaban molestos. La casa aduanal era el lugar donde los británicos recaudaban los impuestos. Esa noche, un solo soldado británico, llamado Hugh White, resguardaba la casa aduanal.

El enojado grupo de jóvenes insultó y le tiró bolas de nieve al soldado. Varios soldados británicos vinieron al auxilio del soldado White. Uno de los jóvenes golpeó a un soldado británico con un palo. Las campanas de las iglesias de Boston comenzaron a sonar para alertar a la gente que había peligro. Como por lo regular las campanas anunciaban un incendio, muchas personas cogieron sus cubetas pensando que una casa se incendiaba. Los soldados británicos escucharon que entre la multitud alguien grito, "¡Fuego!" Los soldados apuntaron sus pistolas muskets al grupo de jóvenes y les dispararon. Tres de los jóvenes murieron en ese momento y dos fallecieron más tarde. Este suceso lo conocemos como "La masacre de Boston." A raíz de este evento aumento el disgusto de los colonos hacia los británicos.

NEWCOMER/BEGINNER	INTERMEDIATE	ADVANCED	NEARLY FLUENT
Students read a more complex and detailed passage about the topic in their native language first, then read 2-3 sentences about the same topic in English. When discussing their reading with a partner, students may default to their native language if the peer is also fluent. Students should be able to summarize their learning in one simple English sentence at the end. *I read about...*	Students read the same complex and detailed passage about the topic in their native language to beginner students first, then read a more condensed version of the passage provided to advanced students. If possible, it is helpful to pair them with advanced or nearly fluent students for the discussion portion. Intermediate students should be encouraged to speak in English during the discussion.	Students read a slightly adapted text that conveys the same information being read by nearly fluent and non-ELL students. It should be similar in length to theirs, with slightly simplified vocabulary and/or definitions of key terms alongside it. Students may be paired with any classmates for the discussion portion.	Students should read the same passage as non-ELL classmates. They should be paired with advanced or non-ELL partners for the discussion portion.

Highlighting PLUS *(Motley, 2016)*

As students read the academic text to accompany the lesson's lecture, they are given a purpose for highlighting key information and an expectation of explaining their reasoning.

> "Your purpose for reading is to evaluate the persuasiveness of the author's argument. While you read, think about whether you are agreeing or disagreeing with her statements. You must highlight at least two arguments and explain their effectiveness."

NEWCOMER/BEGINNER	INTERMEDIATE	ADVANCED	NEARLY FLUENT
Students read a short (2-3 paragraphs) passage in their native language and a shorter text (single paragraph) in English. Students then list the translations for 2-3 key terms.	Students read an adapted text in English comprised of simple and predictable syntax, grammar, and vocabulary. Students highlight two key ideas and record their thinking next to the ideas.	Students read a slightly adapted text that explains key vocabulary in context and complete the Highlighting PLUS strategy for three ideas. Students write 1-2 sentences to summarize the passage.	Students read an on-level text and highlight three ideas. Notes about their thinking for each idea demonstrate complete thoughts, clarity, and precision of language. Students summarize the passage in 2-3 grammatically correct sentences.

Scanning *(Seidlitz & Perryman, 2010a)*

Students scan through a text backward in search of unfamiliar terms. The teacher provides an "in the moment" definition or explanation of the term that aids in comprehension.

Which terms were least familiar to you?

How else could you describe this term?

NEWCOMER/BEGINNER	INTERMEDIATE	ADVANCED	NEARLY FLUENT
Students are provided with a list of key terms to locate in the text, then find native language equivalents to increase understanding.	After the teacher has explained the chosen terms, students may utilize a peer or native-language resource to check for understanding as needed.	Students are able to discuss their predictions for what terms might mean before the teacher provides an explanation. *The term ____ is unfamiliar to me. I think it might mean...*	Students are able to discuss their predictions for what terms might mean before the teacher provides an explanation. *The term ____ is unfamiliar to me. Perhaps it means...*

CHAPTER 4
Show What You Know

✔ Academic Writing

✔ Academic Conversation

Academic writing is a way for students to find and share their "voices," thus highlighting the connections they have made with the material while learning. Academic conversation not only provides a structured opportunity for students to talk about what they've learned, but also cultivates lasting bonds with their classmates.

ACADEMIC WRITING

Whether it is a short formative assessment, an exit ticket, or a formal essay, the writing students do in your classroom showcases their understanding of the content that has been presented and the connections they have made to themselves, their world, and to prior learning. Moreover, encouraging students to find their own voice and share it with others is a useful practice that benefits them long after they leave your classroom.

Academic writing within social studies can be divided into two main categories: writing a clear explanation and making a claim with evidence. Students certainly need these skills in all content areas, but they are essential for communicating their learning in social studies. Students can use either approach to clarify their thinking for themselves and for their audience. They can show you what was most impactful or interesting from the day's lesson. They can provide a window into their thinking and they can expose any misconceptions that might remain.

Making a Clear Explanation: Ways to Expand and Explain Thinking

Type	Description	Questions to ask myself
Facts	Provide true statements about the topic.	What would a Wikipedia entry about this topic say?
Details	Tell more about the topic. Answer: Who? What? When? Where? Why?	What information would the reader need to know about this topic? What is interesting about this topic? What else do I know about the topic?
Example/ Non-example	Show what belongs within the topic and what belongs outside of the topic. Provide a sample that illustrates the topic.	Can I describe a situation that shows what I am trying to explain? What are specific examples of this topic?
Steps	Write information that tells what to do in a specific order.	What should the reader do next? Am I missing any steps?
Definitions/ Description	Tell what something means.	Do I need to explain any of the words in the writing?
Assumptions	Offer information about the topic that seems very basic and obvious.	What do I expect the reader to already know about the topic? What is the most basic information about this topic?

(Motley, 2016)

Making a Claim with Evidence:
Ways to Expand and Explain Thinking

Type	Description	Questions to ask myself
Facts/ Specific Details	Offer true statements about the claim. Give concrete information about the topic. Answer: Who? What? When? Where? Why?	What facts prove my thinking? What information will help to convince my audience that I am correct? What are the reasons for my claim? Why do I think my claim is right?
Statistics	Provide measurable, observable, quantifiable data related to the claim. Record numerical information about the claim.	Do I have any percentages, numbers, graphs, or other data that support my claim?
Examples	Illustrate the claim with a specific event, idea, person, etc.	What specific examples help me prove my claim? Has someone already made the same claim as I am making?
Expert Opinion/ Authority	Provide statements or opinions from a source that has extensive knowledge of the topic.	What do the people who know the most about this topic have to say about the claim? Is there any previous research supporting the claim?

(Motley, 2016)

Academic writing presents several challenges for ELLs, such as difficulty with spelling unfamiliar words, a tendency to use less formal vocabulary, a lack of confidence, native language interference, and the need to "find their voice" in a new language. That might seem like quite a lot to overcome, but the rewards are so clearly worth the effort.

Students who write academically in social studies are able to engage in low-stress language output that truly shows what they know. This helps them make sense of the new content being learned and also accelerates their learning of English in general.

This is the component of your lesson where students' varying proficiency levels will be most evident. For your beginner and intermediate students, the focus should be on expressing their ideas without a lot of specific feedback. Students at these stages of English development should focus on becoming comfortable with how the language works in general by paying attention to phonetics, tone, and basic structures such as how to phrase a question or convey emotion.

Mentor texts and rubrics can be very helpful for your ELLs. Students will write better summaries, for example, after they've been exposed to numerous high-quality examples. A simple rubric can help them focus on a particular skill and can give them insight into how the piece should look when they are finished.

Fortune/Misfortune *(Seidlitz & Perryman, 2010a)*

Students write from a first-person perspective while incorporating both positive and negative events into their academic writing.

1. Have students conduct a "Search and Share" (see page 19) to find as much information about a historical topic as they can in 2-3 minutes.

2. Have students share out the information in a whole-class "Whip Around" (see page 19).

3. Have each group of students brainstorm two fortuitous things that could happen in the context of that historical event, as well as two unfortunate events that might occur. Write each of these events on separate index cards.

4. Collect the finished index cards of fortunes and misfortunes into one deck, then have each student begin an individual piece of writing. For example, if students are writing about the Oregon Trail, they might choose to view themselves as a teenager writing a letter to someone back home.

How would this event affect you?

Who would have a different perspective?

5. Have students write a short paragraph (2-3 sentences) from this first-person perspective describing a typical day in their life from the chosen historical context, using information compiled during the Whip Around.

6. Select a fortune or misfortune card randomly from the deck.

7. Ask students to incorporate the new information into their writing. After they've had time to write a sentence or two, select another card for them to incorporate into their writing.

8. After several cards, ask students to conclude their writing and share with a partner or their group.

NEWCOMER/BEGINNER	INTERMEDIATE	ADVANCED	NEARLY FLUENT
Students use a native-language resource to draw and explain one positive outcome and one negative outcome that could occur in the activity. Students complete one simple English sentence for both positive and negative and include their drawings. *I think _____ is good.* *I think _____ is bad.*	Students' writing should maintain the "voice" chosen at the beginning of the exercise. Because the focus is on content and not structure, it is expected that students will have frequent errors, particularly in terms of verb tense and vague pronouns.	Students' writing should be relatively accurate in terms of verb tense and word choice. Students may not exhibit much abstract thinking due to the "in the moment" nature of the writing task.	Students should compose pieces that are grade-level appropriate with minimal errors that result from unfamiliar contexts. While their pieces may be shorter than those of non-ELL classmates, the quality of the work should be similar. However, since this is a "quick write" without opportunity for revision, more frequent errors than normal are to be expected.

Example/Non-Example *(Motley, 2016)*

The teacher provides students with a high-quality example of the assigned writing, along with an example that does not meet the expectations for that exercise. The class works together to identify what makes the example one to imitate, and why the non-example is not what is desired.

> Do you agree with the reasons the Colonists cited for rebelling against the British Parliament?

✔ Example

I disagree with some of the reasons the colonists were rebelling against the British Parliament, but agree with others. Taxation without representation doesn't seem to be fair. If a government is going to require citizens to pay money, they should give them a chance to be involved in the government. On the other hand, I don't think it was right for the colonists to try to ...

✗ Non-Example

Yes. I didn't like the way that people were doing things. They shouldn't take things for taxes without it being fair. The mercantilism wasn't good for them it wasn't the way it was supposed to be, that's why they got mad about the things that happen. The Boston Massacre and Quartering Soldiers. So I think I agree about them fighting them because ...

What were some of the causes of the American Revolution?

✔ Example

There were a variety of causes of the American Revolution. One cause of the American Revolution was the British policy of taxing the colonists without allowing them to have representatives in Parliament. This angered the colonists because they believed they should be able to have their point of view heard if they were going to be taxed. Another cause was related to the effects of the French and Indian War...

✗ Non-Example

Mercantilism, French and Indian War, and other things. I think it was important to have the war because people were mad at the way the others were acting. The taxing without representing made them mad too. Boston Massacre and Boston Tea Party also...

NEWCOMER/BEGINNER	INTERMEDIATE	ADVANCED	NEARLY FLUENT
Beginning-level writers are not equipped to evaluate English-language samples, so they should be allowed to observe more than participate in this activity. It would be helpful to convey the purpose of the activity through the use of native-language support, such as native-language text on the same topic as the example.	Students would benefit from additional support, such as native-language text on the same topic as the example after the exercise to clarify expectations and "where to start." They could be encouraged to focus on expressing two or three concise ideas in their writing or on maintaining proper verb tenses, for example.	Students should be encouraged to use a variety of sentence structures and to convey complete thoughts in their writing after this exercise.	Students can be expected to convey their thoughts with clarity on a level commensurate with their native English-speaking peers and should be encouraged to focus on supporting their thoughts with evidence where applicable.

RAFT (Role, Audience, Format, Topic) *(Fisher & Frey, 2007)*

Students write from various points of view, audiences to whom they are writing, formats for the writing, and topics within the content.

1. Through assignment or choice, or a combination thereof, students are given a role, audience, format, and topic for their writing.

2. Depending on the purpose for the writing, the teacher might choose to standardize one or more of the components. For example, all students could be asked to write about the same topic, using the same format, and for the same audience. However, they could be assigned different roles. In another instance, students might be asked to write from the same role, on the same topic, and in the same format, but to different audiences.

"What message would be the most important for the person in your role to convey?"

"What would be the ideal reaction for your audience to have?"

Role	Audience	Format	Topic
Urban citizen	Mayor	Letter	*The need for a city-wide recycling program*
Andrew Jackson	U.S. Treasury	Speech (transcribed)	*Why he should not have been replaced on the $20 bill*
Registered voter	Unregistered voter	Email	*The local voter registration process*

3. At the end of the writing process, students should share their work with at least one classmate.

NEWCOMER/BEGINNER	INTERMEDIATE	ADVANCED	NEARLY FLUENT
The scope of this activity might not be clear to beginner students, so it is helpful to keep the structure consistent the first few times they complete a RAFT assignment. Although the topic will change, giving them a standard point of view, audience, and format allows them to focus on content rather than structure. They should be provided a sample with key terms missing and should be able to place the proper terms in the proper blanks.	Students will be more comfortable writing to a familiar audience, such as the teacher or peers, and in a less formal format. They do not require modification of the POV or topic. They should be challenged to write in the formal register occasionally in order to progress into the advanced range.	Students should be encouraged to write in less familiar formats and to less familiar audiences. They should be expected to produce writing that is relatively error-free. They should be able to identify how changing the RAFT elements alters the writing that is produced.	Students should be able to complete this activity at the same level as their non-ELL peers. Errors should be minimal and the tone of the piece should be appropriate for the audience.

When your students have a structured conversation about an academic topic, it is a form of academic discourse. Giving your students time to talk about what they have learned that day helps them to make sense of the new learning and also fosters a sense of community in your classroom.

Open-ended discussion can be intimidating for ELLs. Sometimes students don't know where to start or how to clearly express their thoughts. Using strategies that build in wait time, structures that determine who speaks when, and stems or starters that give students a place to begin, all go a long way in putting your students at ease.

Sentence Stem/Language Scenario:

When my son Andrew was seven years old, we took a family vacation to LEGOLAND in San Diego. Andrew and I are huge LEGO fans, to the extent that our "reward" for missing time together (when I travel to work with other teachers) is to buy a large LEGO set after a certain number of my trips. We build often, enjoying the challenge of more complex kits and the friendly competition we have to be the first to find just the right piece.

Even though the park is designed for children around his age, I could not honestly say which of us was more excited as we waited for the park gates to open on that perfect June day. But, when they did, he made a beeline for the biggest roller coaster in the park. Given that LEGOLAND was designed for 7-11 year olds, this coaster was certainly not an intimidating behemoth by any stretch of the imagination. Still, it was to be his first rollercoaster and I found myself in a terrifying scenario I now know to be quite common in parenting: my child was extremely eager to take on something that I knew might just as easily end in disaster as triumph, possibly leaving him traumatized for life.

It turns out I needn't have worried, because as we made our way down the last "big" descent of the coaster, my snaggle-toothed, newly-fearless son threw his hands in the air and yelled at the top of his lungs, "Based on what is happening right now, I love roller coasters!"

I had to give him a chance to catch his breath before I turned and asked just what in the world had caused him to say exactly that sentence in exactly that way. He informed me that in his kindergarten science class, whenever they completed an investigation, they would use the stem "Based on _____, I..." to share their conclusions. He internalized that sentence starter to the point that it came out organically, over a year later, at one of the happiest moments of his short life, and it made me think: What similar kinds of thoughts will our ELLs express in our classrooms when they have this kind of linguistic support?

T-Chart, Pair, Defend *(Seidlitz & Perryman, 2010a)*

The class works together to create a T-Chart depicting opposing viewpoints about the lesson's topic. Students are assigned a role and use a stem to present the side they have been assigned or use their own words to make their points.

Setting the Stage: Two African-Americans work in a restaurant in Montgomery. They are discussing whether or not to participate in the upcoming bus boycott.

Shared Writing Component: The class works together to come up with three reasons why the workers should participate in the boycott, along with three reasons why they would be reluctant or even opposed to participating in the boycott.

I support the bus boycott because...	I do not support the bus boycott because...
1.	1.
2.	2.
3.	3.

The students then complete a second T-Chart, this time from the perspective of a white business owner. They list three reasons why the business owner might be supportive of the boycott, alongside three reasons why he might be opposed.

I support the bus boycott because...	I do not support the bus boycott because...
1.	1.
2.	2.
3.	3.

Students are placed in pairs. Beginning as the restaurant employees, one partner shares the view of the supporting side, while the other offers reasons to oppose the protest.

The students find new partners and repeat the discussion process, this time posing as white business owners.

Why might you participate in the boycott?

Why might you be reluctant or even opposed to participating?

Finally, students are given the option to choose a role and a viewpoint. They then find a partner with an opposing viewpoint, and discuss the issue using the reasons that have been provided by the T-Charts.

After students have paired with several different partners, they return to their seats and write about the issue from the role and position of their choosing.

Have students choose from the following stems (ranging from minimal to high levels of scaffolding, moving left to right respectively).

Dear Editor,

The bus boycott...

Dear Editor,

I think the bus boycott...

Segregation...

In conclusion...

Dear Editor,

We should/should not support the bus boycott because...

In addition...

Also...

Finally...

NEWCOMER/BEGINNER	INTERMEDIATE	ADVANCED	NEARLY FLUENT
The class T-Chart doubles as a script that students can follow to share the perspective they have been assigned. Beginners are able to read their side of the chart to their partner but are unable to adjust the message.	Students should be able to fluently read aloud their side of the chart. These students will likely use the stems provided.	Students may use the stems but will often use their own words. They should be able to elaborate slightly beyond what is on the chart.	Students can be expected to perform at the same level as non-ELL students in this task.

QSSSA (Question, Signal, Stem, Share, Assess)
(Seidlitz & Perryman, 2010a)

This strategy helps students use new academic language during their conversation. The teacher asks the essential question that will be addressed in the conversation. Students give a signal when they are ready to respond and are given a sentence stem to use for their response. After sharing with a partner, students are chosen randomly to share with the whole group.

Question: Ask the class a question.

Signal: Ask students to give you a response signal when they are ready to answer the question.

Stem: Provide students with a sentence stem to use when answering a question.

Share: Give students an opportunity to share their responses with other students in pairs, triads, or groups.

Assess: Determine the quality of student discussions and the level of understanding by randomly selecting students to share out loud or by having all students write a response.

Question	Signal	Stem	Share	Assess
Do you support Sam Houston's position on secession? Why?	Thinker's Chin*	I support/ oppose Sam Houston's position because…	Numbered Heads Together**	Exit Ticket

*Thinker's Chin: Students put their fists on their chins to indicate they are thinking, then remove their fists when they are ready to respond.

**Numbered Heads Together: Students discuss ideas in groups. Each person in the group is assigned a number. When the teacher solicits responses, he/she picks a specific number to answer for each group. For example, "Will the number three person in each group please stand up?" (Kagan, 1992).

What did your partner share with you?

How were your responses similar/different?

NEWCOMER/BEGINNER	INTERMEDIATE	ADVANCED	NEARLY FLUENT
Students should be able to complete the sentence stem **after** working with their partners. They should not be expected to speak in front of the whole group unless they volunteer.	Students should be able to complete the stem before working with a partner. The share portion should help them clarify their thinking. They might need to be reminded the stem is available when sharing with the whole group.	Students can be expected to perform like non-ELL students in this task. They might choose to use their own words instead of the stem.	Students can be expected to perform like non-ELL students in this task. They might choose to use their own words instead of the stem that is provided.

Expert/Novice *(Seidlitz & Perryman, 2010a)*

Students are divided into pairs. One student takes on the role of an expert and the other a novice in a particular situation. The expert responds to questions asked by the novice, modeling academic language.

1. Have pairs of students brainstorm a list of possible questions they might have about the topic. You can also conduct a whole-class discussion of possible questions to ensure that particular key concepts are included on the list.

2. Have partners prepare a short role-play where one student is the novice who doesn't know anything about the topic. The other student is the expert whose job it is to teach the novice about the topic and to clarify any misconceptions.

3. Provide the following sentence starters to support partners as they create their role-plays:

> **Novice:** *How do you...?*
> *What is...?*
> *I don't understand why...*

> **Expert:** *The first step is...*
> *It is important to...*
> *Let me clarify that...*

4. Choose partners randomly to role-play for the whole class.

Can you explain why...?

Please clarify your statement about...

NEWCOMER/BEGINNER	INTERMEDIATE	ADVANCED	NEARLY FLUENT
Students will be more comfortable in the novice role and should be given questions to ask their partner. They may be able to express the gist of their partner's message in a drawing, in a simple English stem, or as a more detailed retelling in their native language.	Students can serve in either role for this strategy but may face challenges with maintaining academic language throughout the exercise. They are able to summarize the gist of their partner's message as the expert. *My partner said...*	Students benefit from being the expert in this exercise because it is an opportunity to practice academic language. As novices, they can help intermediate students craft their answers to sound more like an expert.	Students can serve in either role. As a novice, they would benefit from a non-ELL or advanced/nearly fluent partner as the expert. When working with an intermediate student, the nearly fluent ELL will benefit most as the expert. Partnering a nearly fluent ELL with a beginner can be frustrating for both partners.

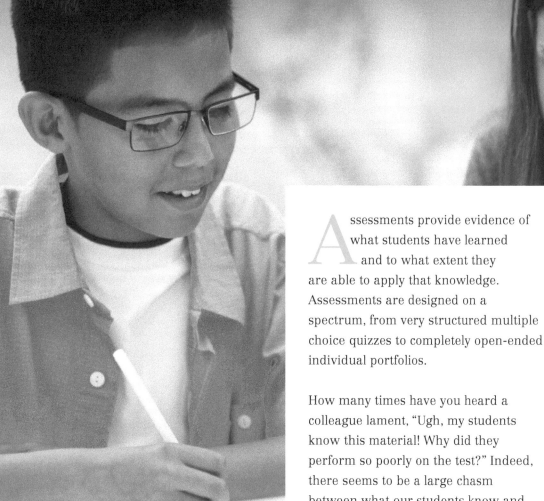

CHAPTER 5
Assessment

Assessments provide evidence of what students have learned and to what extent they are able to apply that knowledge. Assessments are designed on a spectrum, from very structured multiple choice quizzes to completely open-ended individual portfolios.

How many times have you heard a colleague lament, "Ugh, my students know this material! Why did they perform so poorly on the test?" Indeed, there seems to be a large chasm between what our students know and what our test results show. This is even more pronounced for our ELLs. Quite often, ELLs bring more knowledge in their native language than they are able to convey on a structured, English language exam. While these exams provide important information about a student's progress and should be utilized to target instruction and celebrate gains, classroom-based assessments that are given in a different format can go a long way in mitigating some of the frustration felt by students and teachers alike when standardized exams fail to demonstrate the full scope of a student's knowledge.

ADAPTED DBQ (DOCUMENT-BASED QUESTIONS)

The ability to develop a position on an issue after analysis of the evidence is a crucial skill that can be strengthened in every academic discipline. As you may have noticed in recent years, there has been a particular emphasis in this practice in social studies curriculum. When you consider that the desired outcome of a DBQ is for students to think critically, to make connections across sources, and finally to craft a quality written response, the connection to our content is clear. With a few tweaks, teachers can ensure that their ELLs are able to demonstrate as much knowledge as possible during the activity.

Applying a modified gradual release approach to a DBQ is one way to adapt the assessment that is especially beneficial for ELLs at the lower level of proficiency.

1. The class analyzes the question together, with the teacher guiding the discussion. The teacher makes sure the entire question is addressed and that students are moving in the right direction for analysis.

2. Students work in small groups to analyze an individual document and determine how it relates to the question and could be of use in the essay.

3. One by one, groups share their analyses of their documents. This provides a preview of each document that is helpful for ELLs. Before taking on the document themselves, they are able to hear a summary and analysis from their peers. They may also "see" connections between documents that they might have missed if their attention had been focused on reading the information for themselves.

4. Students complete the writing portion individually. For advanced and nearly fluent ELLs, the same evaluation rubric that will be used for their non-ELL peers is appropriate. To adapt the rubric for lower levels of proficiency, consider adjusting the points to focus on addressing the question, presenting a position, and using information from the documents to support the argument.

5. The standard expected outcome from a DBQ is not a realistic goal for beginner and intermediate ELLs. By adapting the scoring process to simply measure how well they addressed the question, crafted an argument, and supported that position with evidence, teachers are able to bring in linguistic goals as well. Teachers can refer to resources, such as the Proficiency Level Descriptors, to determine what a reasonable writing goal would be for these students. Students should be provided the adjusted rubric before writing begins and should be allowed time to edit their responses before submission. Setting secondary linguistic goals solves for two challenges: it provides a differentiated assessment that meets an individual need and it keeps students engaged in the process who might otherwise finish much earlier than their peers.

Example

"Marco, here's your rubric for today's DBQ. I'd like to go over it to make sure you don't have any questions. First, you're going to respond to the question using the strategies we've learned in class. After you're finished, though, I'd like to see you go back and look at the last column on your rubric. It talks about using the right tense of your verbs. So if the sentence is talking about something in the past, the action word in your sentence should be in the past as well. That's something you'll be working on this year as you learn more English."

If the time spent in groups discussing and sharing out is not an option due to the standardized nature of the assignment, it is helpful for ELLs to go through the process with just two documents that clearly contrast. An example is two short entries about a recent Presidential appointment, one from a more left-leaning source, and one from a more conservative viewpoint. It is important to review what linguistic accommodations are allowed in your district and to adapt your DBQ to best showcase what your students know about the topic.

The main goal of a Section Review is to make sure students have learned the key points in the section/chapter and are ready to move forward. Due to the classroom-based nature of this task, it can be conducted in a rather informal way. However, we still need evidence of each student's thinking at the end in order to be sure the class is ready to move on to the next historical milestone.

Here are a few ways we can check for understanding:

1. Quiz, Quiz, Trade: Students are given a notecard and assigned a short portion of the section/chapter. Each student writes a question based on his/her section and writes the answer to the question on the back of the card. After the teacher checks each question, students engage in quizzing each other in pairs. In every partnership, the students trade cards before moving on to the next partner. This helps students hear and read many different questions instead of becoming an expert in just the question they crafted.

   - Beginners should be provided with a card or asked to copy a question that has already been written by the teacher.

   - Intermediate students who have just recently moved up from beginner level can be asked to define bold academic vocabulary in lieu of crafting a question from scratch.

2. Students can be assigned a particular section or paragraph and draw a visual that represents what transpired in that section. The cards can then be arranged in sequential order, as cause-and-effect relationships, and in many other ways. Additionally, displaying particularly effective cards somewhere in your room or awarding a small prize to the best card encourages students to do their best.

3. Turn the section or chapter review questions into a gallery walk. Place each question at the top of a piece of chart paper and give each group of students (3-4 per group) a different color of marker. As they move around the room, students address the question using their colors. They can add to, delete, or modify any previous entries or write a completely new entry. It is helpful to determine what markings will be allowed before the exercise begins so that students can delete information without rendering it illegible, for example.

4. The QSSSA strategy discussed previously in this book can also be used to address the key review questions. Using the questions as the Q, the teacher need only devise a couple of stems and ways for students to share and assess. Interactive resources can be useful for grouping students and for collecting their responses.

5. Assign each student (or each group of 3-4 students) a question from the section or chapter review to answer. Then, have each member of the group convert his/her answer into a text message they would send a friend. Students can then get up and share their texts in partners.

ACCOMMODATED TESTS

The extent to which you can change assessments to make them more appropriate for your ELLs depends on district, state, and federal policies that change from time to time. Additionally, some accommodations that are encouraged in daily instruction may not be available during state testing. It is helpful to work with your campus and district testing staff to be informed about what is allowable so that you can begin to offer those supports well in advance of any standardized assessment. For example, students will be more likely to take advantage of a dictionary during testing if it has been a regular classroom practice and the student is familiar with the particular format. Conversely, students are unlikely to get up during a test and go retrieve an unfamiliar resource stacked in the corner of the silent and still classroom.

There is significantly more flexibility in designing classroom assessments, so teachers are encouraged to assess students in the ways that will be most effective for them to showcase their learning. One of the best ways to find the format that works for them is to ask your students directly. They know what they know and they know how they like to communicate. Why not use the latter to get to the former?

Language Proficiency Differentiation Guide

Warm-Ups

Uncover the Picture

Language Anticipation Guide

Prediction Café

Building Background

List, Group, Label

Search and Share

Describe, Describe, Draw

Interactive Lecture

Turn and Tell Five

Point and Talk

Quick Draw

Academic Reading

Adapted/ Native Language Text

Highlighting PLUS

Scanning

Academic Writing

Fortune/Misfortune

Example/Non-Example

RAFT (Role, Audience, Format, Topic)

Academic Conversation

T-Chart, Pair, Defend

QSSSA (Question, Signal, Stem, Share, Assess)

Expert/Novice

Warm-Up

ACTIVITY	NEWCOMER/BEGINNER	INTERMEDIATE	ADVANCED	NEARLY FLUENT
Uncover the Picture The teacher presents an image on PowerPoint or via document camera that is completely covered. The image is uncovered slowly, as students list things they see.	Students identify items using a native-language resource. *I see a...*	Students identify items and add a descriptor. *I noticed a...*	Students identify items, then add how and why. **It is significant that ____ because...**	Students identify items/ideas, then make predictions. **I'm wondering _____ because...**
Language Anticipation Guide Students are presented with academic terms and phrases that will be discussed in the day's lesson alongside possible definitions of the terms. Students select whether the stated definition (e.g. "the word 'interest' means something that you like or enjoy doing") is the true definition for the way the term is being used in the day's lesson. After instruction, students revisit their initial predictions of what the words meant to see if they need to adjust any of their predictions.	Students complete 1-2 items from each column using a native-language resource for support. *I choose (true/false) for number 1.*	Students complete both columns with teacher support as needed for non-key terms. They discuss any adjustments made to "before" statements using the stem: *I chose (true/false) for number ___, but now I think...*	Students complete both Before and After columns with minimal assistance. They discuss any adjustments made to "before" predictions after reading using the stem: **At first I thought number ___ was (true /false) but now I think ____ because...**	Students complete both Before and After columns without assistance. They discuss any adjustments made to "before" predictions after reading using the stem: **After reading, I changed my answer on number ___ to (true/false) based on...**
Prediction Café The teacher selects quotes, headings, and captions from a text and writes them on cards. Students read/discuss their cards in rotating partnerships, making predictions about the upcoming text/lesson based on their cards. (Even though some students may receive the same card, their predictions will vary.)	Students read a simple caption to each of their partners. *My card says...* *What does yours say?*	After clarification of pronunciation of key terms, students complete this activity without further accommodation. *My card says____, so I predict...*	Students use stems with past, present, and future tenses. *According to my card, (reads card); therefore, my prediction was...*	Students use stems with past, present, future tenses, and complex grammar. **Based on this (caption, quote, heading) that said_____, it is my prediction that_____ (will/will not) ____.**

Building Background

ACTIVITY	NEWCOMER/BEGINNER	INTERMEDIATE	ADVANCED	NEARLY FLUENT
List, Group, Label Students organize vocabulary in a variety of ways to gain a deeper understanding of academic terms to help them clarify the relationships between academic concepts and the meaning of academic terms. Students write key terms on individual cards and then sort the terms into group-generated categories such as topic, characteristic, etc.	Students utilize a native-language resource to find equivalent terms for the academic terms on the cards, placing the English term and a picture on one side and the native language equivalent on the other side. The students then listen to the group discussion, sorting their own cards accordingly.	After clarification of pronunciation of key terms, students share at least one idea during the group discussion.	Students are able to explain the reasoning for the category generated using correct sentence structure and grammar. *We elected to create the category of ____ because...*	Students are able to explain the reasoning for the categories generated using correct sentence structure and grammar. *We elected to create the category of ____ because...*
Search and Share Students are given three minutes to gather as much information as possible (in any language) regarding the day's topic. They then share with their group, compiling a list of all of their answers. This is then followed by a whole class Whip Around.	Students read independently about the topic in their native language, complete a Quick Draw (see p. 23) to show one idea from the reading, and listen to the group and class discussions.	Students read independently about the topic in their native language, English, or a combination of both. They share at least one idea in the group discussion, utilizing the following stem: *One thing I read about (the topic) was ____.*	Students read independently in English and have 3-5 items to share at the end of the time limit. *I discovered ____.*	Students read independently in English and have 3-5 items to share at the end of the time limit. *I discovered ____.*
Describe, Describe, Draw This is a simple three-step strategy that teachers can use to build vocabulary in content-area classes. It gives students multiple exposures to new academic vocabulary and allows them to learn from their peers as well as their teachers.	Students listen attentively to discussions, then utilize a native-language resource to find equivalent terms for the academic terms being discussed. They then draw the English term and a picture on one side and the native language equivalent on the other side.	Students utilize simple sentence stems to participate in the group discussion, and complete the individual/pair discussion with assistance from native-language peer/resource as needed. *I drew a ____ because...*	Students draw a card individually and then share with a peer, collaborating to make any changes or additions.	Students draw a card individually and then share with a peer, collaborating to make any changes or additions.

Interactive Lecture

ACTIVITY	NEWCOMER/BEGINNER	INTERMEDIATE	ADVANCED	NEARLY FLUENT
Turn and Tell Five During the lecture, students are prompted to turn and tell a partner what is being discussed for approximately five seconds. A student is then chosen randomly to share out.	Students speak to a native-language peer, or an English-speaking peer who is comfortable working with a beginner.	Students share with a native-language partner if possible, and likely use a mix of English and native language. *We are discussing...*	Students use a variety of grammatical structures to discuss with a partner. *Today we are discussing ____ because....*	Students use a variety of grammatical structures to discuss with a partner. *Today we are discussing ____ because....*
Point and Talk Before class, the teacher previews the lesson and identifies which directions will be given orally and what key concepts will be discussed. The teacher then plans what objects he/she will hold, refer to, or use as models. While delivering the content, the teacher makes eye contact with students of lower language proficiency levels and occasionally uses questions and response signals to measure understanding of both the content and directions.	Students are instructed in their native language to utilize a series of signals to the teacher to indicate when they need a slower pace or when they would like to talk to a native-language peer or use a resource. Signals such as forming a T with their hands for a time-out to clarify are helpful.	Students use the 1-5 scale when the teacher asks for feedback. They are also prompted to ask for clarification when needed.	Students use the 1-5 scale when the teacher asks for feedback. They are also prompted to ask for clarification when needed.	Students use the 1-5 scale when the teacher asks for feedback. They are also prompted to ask for clarification when needed.
Quick Draw After a key idea has been presented, students are given one minute to quickly sketch a representation of the idea that is then shared with a partner. Finally, a student is chosen randomly to share out before additional volunteers are allowed to share.	Students use a native-language resource and/or peer to complete their sketches.	Students utilize simple sentence stems to discuss their drawings with peers, utilizing native-language peer/resource as needed. *I drew a ____ because...*	Students complete the task individually and then share with a peer, collaborating to make any changes or additions.	Students complete the task individually and then share with a peer, collaborating to make any changes or additions.

Academic Reading

ACTIVITY	NEWCOMER/BEGINNER	INTERMEDIATE	ADVANCED	NEARLY FLUENT
Adapted/Native Language Text Students read a text that is scaffolded for their particular proficiency level, then discuss their reading with a partner.	Students read a more complex and detailed passage about the topic in their native language first, then read 2-3 sentences about the same topic in English. When discussing their reading with a partner, students may default to their native language if the peer is also fluent. Students should be able to summarize their learning in one simple English sentence at the end. *I read about...*	Students read the same complex and detailed passage about the topic in their native language to beginner students first, then read a more condensed version of the passage provided to advanced students. If possible, it is helpful to pair them with advanced or nearly fluent students for the discussion portion. Intermediate students should be encouraged to speak in English during the discussion.	Students read a slightly adapted text that conveys the same information being read by nearly fluent and non-ELL students. It should be similar in length to theirs, with slightly simplified vocabulary and/or definitions of key terms alongside it. Students may be paired with any classmates for the discussion portion.	Students should read the same passage as non-ELL classmates. They should be paired with advanced or non-ELL partners for the discussion portion.
Highlighting PLUS As students read the academic text to accompany the lesson's lecture, they are given a purpose for highlighting key information and an expectation of explaining their reasoning.	Students read a short (2-3 paragraphs) passage in their native language and a shorter text (single paragraph) in English. Students then list the translations for 2-3 key terms.	Students read an adapted text in English comprised of simple and predictable syntax, grammar, and vocabulary. Students highlight two key ideas and record their thinking next to the ideas.	Students read a slightly adapted text that explains key vocabulary in context and complete the Highlighting PLUS strategy for three ideas. Students write 1-2 sentences to summarize the passage.	Students read an on-level text and highlight three ideas. Notes about their thinking for each idea demonstrate complete thoughts, clarity, and precision of language. Students summarize the passage in 2-3 grammatically correct sentences.
Scanning Students scan through a text backward in search of unfamiliar terms. The teacher provides an "in the moment" definition or explanation of the term that aids in comprehension.	Students are provided with a list of key terms to locate in the text, then find native language equivalents to increase understanding.	After the teacher has explained the chosen terms, students may utilize a peer or native-language resource to check for understanding as needed.	Students are able to discuss their predictions for what terms might mean before the teacher provides an explanation. *The term ____ is unfamiliar to me. I think it might mean...*	Students are able to discuss their predictions for what terms might mean before the teacher provides an explanation. *The term ____ is unfamiliar to me. Perhaps it means...*

Academic Writing

ACTIVITY	NEWCOMER/BEGINNER	INTERMEDIATE	ADVANCED	NEARLY FLUENT
Fortune/ Misfortune Students write from a first-person perspective about the academic concept and are faced with making decisions that have a fortunate or unfortunate impact.	Students use a native-language resource to draw and explain one positive outcome and one negative outcome that could occur in the activity. Students complete one simple English sentence for both positive and negative and include their drawings. *I think _____ is good.* *I think _____ is bad.*	Students' writing should maintain the "voice" chosen at the beginning of the exercise. Because the focus is on content and not structure, it is expected that students will have frequent errors, particularly in terms of verb tense and vague pronouns.	Students' writing should be relatively accurate in terms of verb tense and word choice. Students may not exhibit much abstract thinking due to the "in the moment" nature of the writing task.	Students should compose pieces that are grade-level appropriate with minimal errors that result from unfamiliar contexts. While their pieces may be shorter than those of non-ELL classmates, the quality of the work should be similar. However, since this is a "quick write" without opportunity for revision, more frequent errors than normal are to be expected.
Example/Non-Example The teacher provides students with a high quality example of the assigned writing, along with an example that does not meet the expectations for that exercise. The class works together to identify what makes the example one to imitate, and why the non-example is not what is desired.	Beginning-level writers are not equipped to evaluate English-language samples, so they should be allowed to observe more than participate in this activity. It would be helpful to convey the purpose of the activity through the use of native-language support, such as native-language text on the same topic as the example.	Students would benefit from additional support, such as native-language text on the same topic as the example after the exercise to clarify expectations and "where to start." They could be encouraged to focus on expressing two or three concise ideas in their writing or on maintaining proper verb tenses, for example.	Students should be encouraged to use a variety of sentence structures and to convey complete thoughts in their writing after this exercise.	Students can be expected to convey their thoughts with clarity on a level commensurate with their native English-speaking peers and should be encouraged to focus on supporting their thoughts with evidence where applicable.
RAFT (Role, Audience, Format, Topic) Students write from various points of view, audiences to whom they are writing, formats for the writing, and topics within the content.	The scope of this activity might not be clear to beginner students, so it is helpful to keep the structure consistent the first few times they complete a RAFT assignment. Although the topic will change, giving them a standard point of view, audience, and format allows them to focus on content rather than structure. They should be provided a sample with key terms missing and should be able to place the proper terms in the proper blanks.	Students will be more comfortable writing to a familiar audience, such as the teacher or peers, and in a less formal format. They do not require modification of the POV or topic. They should be challenged to write in the formal register occasionally in order to progress into the advanced range.	Students should be encouraged to write in less familiar formats and to less familiar audiences. They should be expected to produce writing that is relatively error-free. They should be able to identify how changing the RAFT elements alters the writing that is produced.	Students should be able to complete this activity at the same level as their non-ELL peers. Errors should be minimal and the tone of the piece should be appropriate for the audience.

Academic Conversation

ACTIVITY	NEWCOMER/BEGINNER	INTERMEDIATE	ADVANCED	NEARLY FLUENT
T-Chart, Pair, Defend The class works together to create a T-Chart depicting opposing viewpoints about the lesson's topic. Students are assigned a role and use a stem to present the side they have been assigned or use their own words to make their points.	The class T-Chart doubles as a script that students can follow to share the perspective they have been assigned. Beginners are able to read their side of the chart to their partner but are unable to adjust the message.	Students should be able to fluently read aloud their side of the chart. These students will likely use the stems provided.	Students may use the stems but will often use their own words. They should be able to elaborate slightly beyond what is on the chart.	Students can be expected to perform at the same level as non-ELL students in this task.
QSSSA This strategy helps students use new academic language during their conversation. The teacher asks the essential question that will be addressed in the conversation. Students give a signal when they are ready to respond and are given a sentence stem to use for their response. After sharing with a partner, students are chosen randomly to share with the whole group.	Students should be able to complete the sentence stem **after** working with their partners. They should not be expected to speak in front of the whole group unless they volunteer.	Students should be able to complete the stem before working with a partner. The share portion should help them clarify their thinking. They might need to be reminded the stem is available when sharing with the whole group.	Students can be expected to perform like non-ELL students in this task. They might choose to use their own words instead of the stem.	Students can be expected to perform like non-ELL students in this task. They might choose to use their own words instead of the stem that is provided.
Expert/Novice Students are divided into pairs. One student takes on the role of an expert and the other a novice in a particular situation. The expert responds to questions asked by the novice, modeling academic language.	Students will be more comfortable in the novice role and should be given questions to ask their partner. They may be able to express the gist of their partner's message in a drawing, in a simple English stem, or as a more detailed retelling in their native language.	Students can serve in either role for this strategy but may face challenges with maintaining academic language throughout the exercise. They are able to summarize the gist of their partner's message as the expert. *My partner said…*	Students benefit from being the expert in this exercise because it is an opportunity to practice academic language. As novices, they can help intermediate students craft their answers to sound more like an expert.	Students can serve in either role. As a novice, they would benefit from a non-ELL or advanced/nearly fluent partner as the expert. When working with an intermediate student, the nearly fluent ELL will benefit most as the expert. Partnering a nearly fluent ELL with a beginner can be frustrating for both partners.

sources

https://en.oxforddictionaries.com/explore/how-many-words-are-there-in-the-english-language

https://www.edutopia.org/big-thinkers-judy-willis-neuroscience-learning-video

http://www.teachtci.com/teaching-strategy-and-classroom-technology-webinars/teaching-with-documents-and-dbqs-without-the-dull-factor.html

http://dbqproject.com

Auer, V., & Hartill, M. (2014). *Vocabulary Now! 44 Strategies All Teachers Can Use.* San Clemente, CA: Canter Press.

Echevarria, J., Vogt, M. E., & Short, D. (2008). *Making Content Comprehensible for English Language Learners: The SIOP Model* (3rd ed.). Boston: Allyn and Bacon.

Fisher, D., & Frey, N. (2007). *Checking For Understanding: Formative Assessment Techniques for Your Classroom.* Alexandria, VA: Association for Supervision and Curriculum Development.

Gibbons, P. (2015). *Scaffolding Language, Scaffolding Learning: Teaching English Language Learners in the Mainstream Classroom* (2nd ed.). Portsmouth, NH: Heinemann.

Head, M., & Readence, J. (1986). Anticipation Guides: Meaning Through Prediction. In E. Dishner, T. Bean, J. Readence, & D. Moore (Eds.), (1986). *Reading in the Content Areas.* Dubuque, IA: Kendall/Hunt.

Kagan, S. (1992). *Cooperative Learning.* San Juan Capistrano, CA: Kagan Cooperative Learning.

Lee, J. F. & VanPatten, B. (2003). *Making Communicative Language Teaching Happen.* Boston: McGraw-Hill.

Marzano, R. (2004). *Building Academic Background.* Alexandria, VA: MCREL, ASCD.

Motley, N. (2016). *Talk, Read, Talk, Write* (2nd ed.). San Clemente, CA: Canter Press.

Seidlitz, J. (2011). *38 Great Academic Language Builders: Activities for Math, Science, Social Studies, Language Arts...and Just about Everything Else.* San Clemente, CA: Canter Press.

Seidlitz, J. (2010a). *ELPS Flipbook: A User Friendly Guide for Academic Language Instruction.* San Clemente, CA: Canter Press.

Seidlitz, J. (2010b). *Navigating the ELPS.* San Clemente, CA: Canter Press.

Seidlitz, J. (2008). *Sheltered Instruction Plus.* San Clemente, CA: Canter Press.

Seidlitz, J., Base, M., Lara, M., & Smith, H. (2016). *ELLs in Texas: What Teachers Need to Know* (2nd ed.). San Clemente, CA: Canter Press.

Seidlitz, J., & Perryman, B. (2010a). *7 Steps to a Language Rich Interactive Classroom.* San Clemente, CA: Canter Press.

Seidlitz, J., & Perryman, B. (2010b). *Navigating the ELPS in the Social Studies Classroom.* San Clemente, CA: Canter Press.

Schleppegrell, M. J. (2004). *The Language of Schooling: A Functional Linguistics Perspective.* NY: Routledge.

Taba, H. (1967). *Teachers' Handbook for Elementary Social Studies.* Reading, MA: Addison-Wesley.

Zwiers, J. (2008). *Building Academic Language.* Newark, DE: Jossey-Bass/International Reading Association.

TINA BEENE is an educational consultant with Seidlitz Education and the creator of the Teaching to ELs series. She previously served as a bilingual social studies teacher, bilingual program coordinator, and secondary ESL facilitator and draws on those experiences in her current roles as a trainer, coach, and author. Tina has also crafted a number of professional development sessions which focus on student engagement, language acquisition, and best practices for classroom instruction.

Three ways to order

- **FAX** completed order form with payment information to **(949) 200-4384**
- **PHONE** order information to **(210) 315-7119**
- **ORDER ONLINE** at **www.seidlitzeducation.com**

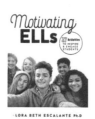

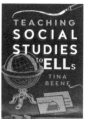

TITLE	PRICE	QTY	TOTAL$	TITLE	PRICE	QTY	TOTAL$
NEW! 7 Steps To a Language-Rich, Interactive **Foreign Language Classroom**	$32.95			7 Pasos para crear un aula interactiva y rica en lenguaje SPANISH	$29.95		
NEW! Boosting Achievement: Reaching Students with Interrupted or Minimal Education	$26.95			38 Great Academic Language Builders	$24.95		
NEW! Motivating ELLs: 27 Activities to Inspire & Engage Students	$26.95			Diverse Learner Flip Book	$26.95		
NEW! Pathways to Greatness for ELL Newcomers: A Comprehensive Guide for Schools & Teachers	$32.95			ELLs in Texas: What Teachers Need to Know 2ND EDITION	$34.95		
NEW! Sheltered Instruction in Texas: Second Language Acquisition Methods for Teachers of ELs	$29.95			ELLs in Texas: What Administrators Need to Know 2ND EDITION	$29.95		
NEW! Talk Read Talk Write: A Practical Routine for Learning in All Content Areas K-12 2ND EDITION	$32.95			ELPS Flip Book	$19.95		
NEW! Teaching Social Studies to ELLs	$24.95			Navigating the ELPS: Using the Standards to Improve Instruction for English Learners	$24.95		
NEW! Teaching Science to English Learners	$24.95			Navigating the ELPS: Math (2nd Edition)	$29.95		
NEW! ¡Toma la Palabra! SPANISH	$32.95			Navigating the ELPS: Science	$29.95		
NEW! Mi Cuaderno de Dictado SPANISH	$7.95			Navigating the ELPS: Social Studies	$29.95		
7 Steps to a Language-Rich Interactive Classroom	$29.95			Navigating the ELPS: Language Arts and Reading	$34.95		
				RTI for ELLs Fold-Out	$16.95		
				Vocabulary Now! 44 Strategies All Teachers Can Use	$29.95		
COLUMN 1 TOTAL $							

COLUMN 2 TOTAL $	
COLUMN 1+2	$
DISCOUNT	$
SHIPPING	$
TAX	$
TOTAL	$

Pricing, specifications, and availability subject to change without notice.

SHIPPING 9% of order total, minimum $14.95
5-7 business days to ship. If needed sooner please call for rates.
TAX EXEMPT? please fax a copy of your certificate along with order.

NAME

SHIPPING ADDRESS   CITY   STATE, ZIP

PHONE NUMBER   EMAIL ADDRESS

TO ORDER BY FAX
to **(949) 200-4384**
please complete
credit card info *or*
attach purchase order

☐ Visa ☐ MasterCard ☐ Discover ☐ AMEX

CARD #   EXPIRES
                                          mm/yyyy
SIGNATURE   CVV
                               3- or 4- digit code

☐ **Purchase Order attached**
please make P.O. out to **Seidlitz Education**

For information about Seidlitz Education products and professional development, please contact us at

(210) 315-7119 | kathy@johnseidlitz.com
56 Via Regalo, San Clemente, CA 92673
www.seidlitzeducation.com

Giving kids the gift of **academic language.**™

REVO61419

SEIDLITZ | PRODUCT ORDER FORM

Three ways to order

- **FAX** completed order form with payment information to **(949) 200-4384**
- **PHONE** order information to **(210) 315-7119**
- **ORDER ONLINE** at **www.seidlitzeducation.com**

Pricing, specifications, and availability subject to change without notice.

TITLE	Price	QTY	TOTAL $
NEW! *Instead Of I Don't Know* Poster For the LOTE Classrom 24" x 36"			
☐ LOTE FRENCH	$9.95		
☐ LOTE SPANISH	$9.95		
☐ LOTE GERMAN	$9.95		
		TOTAL $	

TITLE	Price	QTY	TOTAL $
Instead Of I Don't Know Poster, 24" x 36"			
☐ Elementary ENGLISH	$9.95		
☐ Secondary ENGLISH	$9.95		
20 pack *Instead Of I Don't Know* Posters, 11" x 17"			
☐ Elementary ENGLISH	$40.00		
☐ Secondary ENGLISH	$40.00		
Instead Of I Don't Know Poster, 24" x 36" Elementary SPANISH	$9.95		
20 pack *Instead Of I Don't Know* Posters, 11" x 17" Elementary SPANISH	$40.00		
		TOTAL $	

TITLE	Price	QTY	TOTAL $
Academic Language Cards and Activity Booklet, ENGLISH	$19.95		
Academic Language Cards, SPANISH	$9.95		
		TOTAL $	

TITLE	Price	QTY	TOTAL $
Please Speak In Complete Sentences Poster 24" x 36"			
☐ ENGLISH ☐ SPANISH	$9.95		
20 pack *Please Speak In Complete Sentences* Posters, 11" x 17"			
☐ ENGLISH ☐ SPANISH	$40.00		
		TOTAL $	

SHIPPING 9% of order total, minimum $14.95
5-7 business days to ship.
If needed sooner please call for rates.

TAX EXEMPT? please fax a copy of your certificate along with order.

GRAND TOTAL	$
DISCOUNT	$
SHIPPING	$
TAX	$
FINAL TOTAL	$

NAME

SHIPPING ADDRESS   CITY   STATE, ZIP

PHONE NUMBER   EMAIL ADDRESS

TO ORDER BY FAX to **(949) 200-4384** please complete credit card info *or* attach purchase order

☐ Visa ☐ MasterCard ☐ Discover ☐ AMEX

CARD #   EXPIRES
          mm/yyyy

SIGNATURE   CVV

☐ **Purchase Order**

please make P.O. out to **Seidlitz Education**